WITHDRAWN

D1382630

WITHDRAWN

A
JOURNEY
OF
MADNESS

Part 1

ANNEMARIE BRANT

authorHOUSE®

AuthorHouse™ UK
1663 Liberty Drive
Bloomington, IN 47403 USA
www.authorhouse.co.uk
Phone: 0800 047 8203 (Domestic TFN)
*   +44 1908 723714 (International)*

© 2019 Annemarie Brant. All rights reserved.

No part of this book may be reproduced, stored in a retrieval system, or transmitted by any means without the written permission of the author.

Published by AuthorHouse   07/12/2019

ISBN: 978-1-7283-9076-5 (sc)
ISBN: 978-1-7283-9075-8 (e)

Print information available on the last page.

Any people depicted in stock imagery provided by Getty Images are models, and such images are being used for illustrative purposes only. Certain stock imagery © Getty Images.

This book is printed on acid-free paper.

Because of the dynamic nature of the Internet, any web addresses or links contained in this book may have changed since publication and may no longer be valid. The views expressed in this work are solely those of the author and do not necessarily reflect the views of the publisher, and the publisher hereby disclaims any responsibility for them.

"**M**um! Mum! Mum!"

Annemarie heard her son, Richard, shouting. It was early in the morning. Sighing, she snuggled under the covers, hoping that today would be different.

"Mum! Look, Mum!" he demanded. The covers were ripped away from her face.

Peering up past his mammoth chest, she narrowed her eyes on him. "What, Rich?"

Richard was nineteen years old. He exuded health and vitality—the kind that came from strenuous physical activity. He was also very pissed off, pinning his mum with a hard stare. Enunciating each word, he said, "Look what those tablets have done. Look!"

Confused, Annemarie pushed up into a sitting position and crossed her arms over her chest. After taking a deep breath, she calmed her voice to something a little more human than a growl. "Was there something you wanted?"

Richard's face was grim. His body seemed to swell with aggression. "Those tablets—those fucking tablets—those wanky doctors put me on have given me bitch tits!" he barked. "Fucking look, Mum!" He pointed to his chest.

Annemarie leaned forward, squinting at his chest. She

raised an eyebrow. *What the hell?* she thought. Richard's nipples were indeed red and very puffy. Biting her lower lip and schooling her face into a hesitant, hopeful expression, she murmured, "They look OK."

Richard went completely still. His jaw dropped and then snapped shut. He looked at her with wide, disbelieving eyes. "No, Mum! This is not OK. I've got bitch tits—milky bitch tits. Look! Fucking look! They're like lactating women's tits," he howled, glaring down at his defined pectoral muscles. He snapped his head up and gave her the death stare. "And that's not all," he whispered ominously, clenching his jaw. "My dick doesn't work either."

Annemarie blinked. Her expression was carefully blank.

"Did you hear me, Mum?" he demanded. "My dick—doesn't—work!" Richard pressed his lips together into a grim line, closing his eyes in despair. He turned and started pacing, bunching his fists. He took a deep breath and bellowed, "My fucking dick is limp, Mum! It lies there like a dead fish. I have to slap it to wake it up. That's not right—my dick always works." He turned and glared at Annemarie. Venom dripped from every word as he hissed, "It's those tablets. Those fucking tablets have given me bitch tits and a limp dick. What the fuck, Mum?" He continued to rage.

Suppressing a weary sigh and offering a reassuring smile, she told him that they had an appointment at the hospital that afternoon and they would talk to the doctor about his medication. After shooing him out of the room so she could get washed and dressed, she heard him storm downstairs, muttering to himself.

Annemarie threw her car keys onto the hall table. Richard brushed past her without saying a word. Biting her lip, she watched him run up the stairs. She waited, listening for the loud slam of his bedroom door. She made her way to the kitchen and found her husband, Russell, washing dishes. He turned towards her with a tea towel in his hand. His tired smile warmed her.

"How did it go?" he quietly asked.

Annemarie frowned. She was still mulling over the afternoon's events. "I don't know what's happening, Russell, but it's scary."

The consultant had said that Richard was showing early signs of psychosis. She talked to Richard, reminding him of some of the things he'd been experiencing, like hearing the voice of God, thinking that the car beeping at eight in the morning to collect the next-door neighbour's child was actually a signal to run, and his infatuation with his work colleague. Annemarie leaned against the kitchen counter and crossed her arms. "The consultant explained at length the early warning signs of psychosis and how difficult they are to distinguish from normal young-adult behaviour. However, she thinks that Richard is showing worrisome symptoms." Annemarie took a deep breath and looked up into her husband's eyes. "The consultant said that it's probably been going on for some time and we just didn't pick up on it."

She pushed her hair away from her face. "Do you remember when he was working at Smith's building firm and Anthony called you to say Richard was behaving strangely? Richard was marching up and down the road, shouting and swearing. He was visibly upset. It was so unlike Richard's normal, laid-back personality. It was confusing to both of us. Then, when he was working part-time in the bistro, he started talking about those very strong, inappropriate emotions he felt for that much older woman. And what about these persistent strange thoughts and beliefs that he can't set aside no matter how many times we tell him they're untrue? Well, they are all early signs of psychosis."

Russell reached up for a mug from the shelf and poured her a cup of coffee. Talking over his shoulder, he asked, "Will he get better? Will the antipsychotic drugs cure him?"

She shook her head. "They don't know! The consultant asked Richard if he'd been taking any drugs like marijuana or LSD, and then she asked him if he would agree to a drug test. She asked me if we had any family members with mental health issues. Naturally, I told her no," she said, her voice cracking.

Russell widened his eyes, giving Annemarie a funny look.

"What?" she barked. She knew what he was inferring.

Russell passed Annemarie her coffee, trying to hide a wry smile. He loved to tease her about her bizarre behaviour during her pregnancies. She had become extremely distracted and scatterbrained. Any little thing could trigger an avalanche of emotions which would undoubtedly end up in a bout of weeping that left her face blotchy and her nose red.

Looking slightly miffed, Annemarie stared at him over the rim of her coffee cup, muttering, "Lots of women struggle with pregnancy hormones."

Russell's face turned serious. "So he needs to continue with the medication and keep going to appointments. Is that it?"

She nodded her head, took a breath and held it for

a moment, and then slowly exhaled. "They've changed the antipsychotics to ones that don't have such severe side effects—but yes, continue to take them and try to go on as normal. Richard asked if he could do some work for a friend, landscaping in Beckenham tomorrow. The consultant told him that if he was feeling well and wanted to go, he could. She called it a safe risk."

Abigail and Emily trundled into the kitchen, both trying to grab the last diet cola from the fridge. Annemarie turned to smile at the girls and then pecked Russell on the cheek. "OK—everyone, out. I need to start cooking dinner."

It was a lovely, bright day. Richard got up early, showered, and dressed in shorts and a T-shirt. Terry was picking him up at nine to go to the landscaping job. The job required intense manual labour, hand digging out a giant tree stump in a garden. The work was very physical. Using a shovel, Richard had to dig around the stump until the largest roots were exposed. Terry used a lopper to break up the root system, and then they used shovels to fit underneath and dislodge the stump.

Success! While they were having a tea break, Richard heard the car horn beep. He went very still and on the alert, waiting for it to beep again. He heard a second beep. Like an athlete exploding from the starting block, Richard sprinted through the garden and out of the gate. He ran down the street, made a sharp turn through the alley, and bounded up the steps, arriving at the main road. Cars whizzed past him. He frantically looked to his left and to his right, unsure of what to do next. He slowly turned and retraced his steps back to Terry in the garden. Terry waved at Richard as he came through the gate. Richard looked sweaty and out of breath. His wet T-shirt stuck to his massive frame.

"Where did you go?" Terry asked with a smile.

Richard had been a huge asset in getting the first of the two massive tree stumps out of his client's garden. Richard shrugged and mumbled something about going for a walk.

The second tree stump was bigger than the first. Terry's client had tried to burn it, but his attempts had been unsuccessful. Richard started to dig around the second stump. It was hard going. Richard could hear Terry on his phone in the background, and he didn't sound happy. His voice was tense, and his replies to the caller seemed angry.

"I've got to go out for a bit. Are you OK carrying on your own for ten minutes?" Terry asked Richard.

After nodding and waving off Terry, Richard carried on digging. He stopped when he heard the first beep of a car horn. Richard froze, waiting. There it was—the second beep! Richard threw down the shovel, sprinted through the garden, jumped the garden wall, ran down the street, made his way through the alley, and leapt up the steps. The cars whizzed past him as he got to the main road. He waited a few minutes to catch his breath. Looking at the cars, Richard inhaled deeply, and then he slowly turned and made his way back to the garden. He was just coming through the alley when again he heard the car horn. This time he knew he would make it. He turned and sprinted back to the main road, chasing after the car he thought had sounded its horn. Soon he was surrounded by cars beeping their horns. Drivers yelled at him to get off the road. The noise grew to a cacophony that compelled him to run faster.

He stripped off his T-shirt, threw it away, and took off running.

Two police officers patrolling the neighbourhood tried to intercept him at the corner of High Street. Richard knew they wanted information about Terry. He thought that if he distracted them and got them to chase him, then Terry would have a better chance to get away. Richard knew Terry was in trouble because of the phone call he'd taken earlier in the day. Richard needed to do something criminal to keep the police focused on him, giving Terry a chance to escape.

Jogging now, Richard ducked into a supermarket, grabbed one of the ironing boards close to the exit, and made off with it, carrying it under his arm. It wasn't long before he realised that running with his stolen ironing board was an annoyance. He slow jogged past some cars waiting at the traffic lights, and someone called his name. "Richard! What, you're doing some ironing?" It was Anthony, his old boss from Smith's.

Laughing Richard stood in front of Anthony's car, pretending to iron. Anthony shook his head and shouted, "Get out of the way, you idiot. The lights have turned green."

Enjoying himself now, Richard watched Anthony's car drive off. *Wow, it's hot,* he thought, stripping off his shorts and boxers. He threw them and the ironing board into the bushes. Running naked felt good, powerful …

Emily liked Thursdays because school finished early. She got in, dumped her school bag, and kicked off her school shoes. Then she made her way to the kitchen to get herself a can of cola. The landline phone was ringing. She picked it up.

"Hello, it's the police," the caller said. "Do you know a Richard Brant?"

Emily sucked in her lip, suddenly feeling very apprehensive. "Yes, he's my brother," she replied.

The police had picked up Richard and wanted to know if he had a history of mental health issues. Emily was able to explain that he had recently been seeing a doctor for mental health problems. The police officer gave Emily a phone number and told her that her parents should call them back as soon as possible.

Annemarie parked the car on the driveway, grabbing a few bags of groceries. She looked up with a smile when she saw Emily rushing towards her. The smile died instantly as she took in the distressed look on her daughter's face. "Mum," she cried, "the police phoned. They've got Richard, and they want you to call this number." She thrust the piece of paper into Annemarie's trembling hand. Emily ushered her inside so she could make the call.

"We have Richard," the police officer said. "We've put him on a 136 section for his own safety. We're waiting for an ambulance, and then we'll escort him with the ambulance crew to the hospital. Can you meet us at the hospital?"

Tick, tick, boom! Annemarie put the phone down, trying to keep down the overwhelming panic that rose in her throat, strangling her and constricting her breathing. She knew something had been coming for weeks now, but not knowing the when or the how left her perpetually anxious. She sensed a dark shadow descending over her family, especially over Richard. Her hand covered her mouth to hide her trembling lips. She turned to Emily, giving her some brief instructions to call Dad and hold down the fort.

The drive to the mental hospital at the edge of town took her sixteen minutes. She used the time to force down the panic, taking deep breaths. She needed to stay calm because her son needed her. She had to stay strong. A pathetic, weepy mess wouldn't be helpful, even though it was tempting. At the psychiatric hospital, Annemarie parked the car and went towards the entrance. She marvelled that for years she'd been driving past, not knowing or caring what it was or who had to visit such a place. Well, that all changed three weeks ago, when Richard's strange behaviour became obvious. The automatic doors swished open. Annemarie asked at the reception desk if Richard had arrived. She told the receptionist Richard was coming in on a 136 section. The receptionist peered over her glasses at Annemarie and then ran her fingers down a list of names. Bizarrely, Annemarie thought to herself, *What a strange creature. Middle-aged, bun-wearing shusher in glasses. That's often found in libraries—and also in psychiatric hospitals, apparently.*

A police car pulled up outside the entrance, followed by an ambulance. The back doors of the ambulance opened. Richard looked confused and lost, and he was clearly relieved when he saw his mum hurrying towards him. She ignored the police holding on to his arms, the ambulance crew surrounding him, the handcuffs, and the strange sweatpants and T-shirt. She wrapped her arms round his waist and hugged him. He bent down to rest his head on her shoulder.

She whispered in his ear, "I'm here." Richard straightened and gave his mum a watery smile. Swallowing, she asked, "Are you OK?" Richard nodded.

One of the three officers said, "Come on. Let's go in," and gently guided Richard into the reception, through some double doors, and down corridors until they entered a large room labelled "Assessment suite". The officer removed the handcuffs, and mother and son huddled together on the plastic-coated bench.

It wasn't long before a doctor came in. He wasn't wearing a white coat, was about thirty-five, and was casually dressed. He used a security card to let himself into the suite, making sure it was locked behind him. He approached Richard and his mum, carefully introducing himself as the consultant on duty. After turning to the police, he asked if they could give him a report on what had occurred. The three officers waiting in the room slightly moved at once; it was like a trigger.

In seconds Richard was up, ripping off the loose clothing and roaring, "All right, that's it!"

Richard knew he could have all three officers. They looked weak, unfit, and soft. They would need six people to take him down. Adrenaline rushed through his body, making his muscles swell. He could feel the imminent attack down to his bones. Richard was seized by an overwhelmingly savage impulse to strike, rush at the police, take them down, and deliver some pain. He started to pace, keeping his eyes on his enemies. They were pussies, backing away slowly with hands up, making nonthreatening gestures.

One of the officers got his attention by calling his name and saying, "Sit down, mate. It's OK."

They might be playing me, Richard thought. *Better stay strong, keep fit. Stay strong like Charley Bronson. That's it; give it to 'em, my son. One hundred press-ups fast. That's it, boy. Keep fit, stay strong.*

Annemarie sat in shock. In a daze, she watched her

son's naked, hairy butt flexing as he continued to do press-ups while starkers. She was sure her mouth was open in astonishment. Dumbfounded, she gave a stunned, questioning look at the police and the doctor, who had no answers and simply stared back at her with what looked like mild astonishment. She got to her feet and shakenly followed Richard as he paced towards the door, walking past the officers.

One of them said, "It's locked, Richard. You can't go anywhere yet."

Looking over her shoulder with an "Are you kidding me?" look, she turned to see Richard pull the door once. When it didn't open, he used a strong, fast, forceful jerk. The door popped open, and this set off the alarms. Laughing at the scrambling officers, Richard crowed, "Hey, wankers! Need better doors!"

Running to keep up with Richard, Annemarie was aware of the officers behind them. Suddenly and unexpectedly, Richard stopped, and she ploughed into his unmoveable back. Richard grabbed her to keep her from falling. In front and closing in fast was a pack of female and male nurses. The alarms had caused them to rush to help. Breathlessly Annemarie gasped, "Richard, you're naked. Come on, let's go back."

"Um, OK," he said, and he walked back into the assessment suite like a lamb. She was sure it was the realization that he was naked in front of all the staff that made him have second thoughts.

Richard knew they were against him. He wanted to be ready if they attacked him. He gave them a show of strength, doing press-ups. In his mind, he could hear the encouraging words of Charlie Bronson. He knew he could get out of the room; the locking system was magnetic. *Pathetic, really.* He nodded to himself, chuckling evilly. He could have escaped, and he knew his way out. But Mum was with him, and she looked scared, so he was a good boy for her. The wankers hadn't expected him to be able to force the door open.

The doctor gave him two tablets, and they had a big male nurse, guarding the door now. Richard smirked at him. The doctor and a woman was talking some shit to mum. He didn't care because he felt tired. *One hundred press-ups, fast. Stay fit, stay strong.* Richard paced the long room, eyeing the male nurse up and down. He kept moving, staying alert and waiting for an opportunity to force the door open again. *Just for fun.*

They gave Richard another two tablets. They needed him to calm down because he was a flight risk, they said. Annemarie tried to stay composed, but she was terrified. The duty consultant and female social worker were waiting for another doctor to arrive for his assessment of Richard. If that doctor agreed with the consultant and social worker's assessment, Richard would be detained under the Mental Health Act, on a section 2. He would have to stay on a psychiatric ward for a minimum of twenty-eight days. Annemarie knew they were recording everything that was happening in the assessment suite; she could hear someone typing on a keyboard in the little office. One of the police officers had gone into that room, and she could hear his voice quietly give his account of Richard's mental state when they'd intercepted him earlier. Then when the office door opened wide, she saw on a computer screen her own tightly drawn, white features with Richard slumped next to her.

They had enough footage of Richard ripping his clothes off, doing naked push-ups, and his maniacal laugh to realise something was wrong.

A male nurse showed Richard and Annemarie into a ward. When they got to the double doors, the ward sister stopped Annemarie. "Just him," she said, nodding to Richard. "You can't come in."

Annemarie quickly gave Richard a hug and told him she would see him tomorrow morning. She gave the ward sister a frown. *Thanks for the reassurance, bitch.* Her throat tight with tears, she watched as her son was led into the ward.

While escorting her out of the building, the male duty staff nurse briefly told her that they might move Richard to another hospital in the morning because they didn't have a bed for him. Annemarie looked at him, confused. "He won't be staying here?"

"No, we don't think so. We don't have any beds at the moment. It could be very early in the morning. We'll let you know where we've transferred him."

Shaking her head, she quickly wrote her name and mobile number on his clipboard. "Don't try to move him without me. Call me as soon as it's arranged. He won't want to go without me there." Not convinced, he told her that he would try, but the private ambulance service wouldn't hang around.

Annemarie walked through the empty parking lot, surprised it was dark and deserted. A great wave of helplessness washed over her. Tears held in check for so long flooded her eyes. After getting into her car, she rested her head on the steering wheel and let herself have a moment.

Then with a deep, shuddering breath, she pulled back her shoulders, started the car, and drove home.

At 4 a.m., Annemarie received the call from the duty nurse. Richard was being moved, and they weren't waiting! "It would be best if you visited him at the new hospital tomorrow," he advised.

Annemarie hung up. *Fuck that!* She was already in fresh leggings and top, throwing on an oversized sweater and pushing her feet into pumps. After grabbing purse, keys, and phone, she was in the car in less than a minute. Annemarie drove recklessly through the empty streets, hands tight on the steering wheel. She prayed that she wouldn't be stopped by the police—not because she was afraid of getting into trouble and getting a ticket, but because it would delay her from getting to Richard.

Upon turning into the long, winding driveway that led to the hospital, she was astounded to see her son sprinting towards her with bare feet, still in his borrowed sweats and T-shirt. She could see in the distance that some of the staff were giving chase. Richard was about one hundred meters in front, gritting his teeth in determination. She stopped her car and waited until he was close to shout, "Richard!" indicating he should get in.

Relieved, he shouted back, "Mum!" He threw himself into the passenger seat and shouted "Go, go, go!"

Annemarie was very tempted. She looked at the motley crew of professionals still metres away. She turned to her son and said, "Darling, we're not going anywhere but back there." She indicated the hospital in the distance.

Richard slumped into the seat. "Aww …" The sound of his disappointment was cute, and she had to sympathise with how he felt. They were going to cart him off to goodness knew where. It must have been scary and confusing. He'd been given 20 mg lorazepam the night before, so he was too out of it to really understand anything.

The fastest psychiatric nurse had finally reached her car, bent over with hands on his knees, breathing like a dragon. He tried to speak but ended up coughing his guts up. Richard leant over her to push his face out of the window, hooting with laughter at the nurse's ineptitude. Annemarie found nothing about the situation amusing. Shooting murderous glares at the mental health team, she barked, "I'm his mum. I will drive him back." After putting her car into gear, she drove sedately past the obviously embarrassed but somewhat grateful staff.

She sat in the car with Richard for a few minutes until all the staff arrived back at the entrance of the hospital. He explained that he didn't know where they were taking him, and he didn't want to go without his mum. Annemarie nodded in agreement. He said, "I went with them all nice and quiet until we got outside, and then I gave them the slip."

Richard and Annemarie got out of the car and walked towards the duty staff nurse who had called her to let her know about Richard being transported. He grimaced at the sight of her giving him a death stare. "What's the plan?" she questioned. Annemarie had the address of the hospital in Kent, where they were transporting Richard. The plan was for her to follow behind the private ambulance so she could be with him when he arrived at the new psychiatric hospital. She asked if she could travel in the ambulance too, but they said it was not insured for that.

Richard let them guide him to the private ambulance. He was asked to sit in the steel holding cell at the back of the ambulance, like the ones they had in police vans. Before they closed the back door, locking him into the cell, she reassured Richard she was following behind. She gave him a wave and a smile before quickly turning to get into her car. "The driver called, have you got the address in case you lose us?" She nodded as she jumped into her car, not wanting to be left behind.

Richard was sitting on a little steel seat. He couldn't see his mum following them because the ambulance had solid back doors. The small cell was for one person, and it was a steel box. The door on the inside had six small holes. When he peeked through the holes, he could see a driver and a passenger, both male. It was difficult to stay on the slippery seat. They made their way down the driveway and away from hospital. Then turned onto the wide main road. Suddenly and without any warning, they put on the emergency sirens and increased their speed from thirty miles per hour to what felt like eighty. Richard knew his mum wouldn't keep up because they were driving too fast. *What are they playing at? Are they trying to kidnap me?* "Hey! Hey, stop!" The siren was so loud it hurt his ears. *They can't hear me.* "Slow down!" he shouted again. The men ignored him and continued to speed down the road with the siren blaring. Richard could feel anxiety growing. He had to get out and get them to slow down. He angrily lay on his back in the tight confines of the cell, using his powerful legs to kick the steel door over and over. After three or four kicks, it was nearly bent in half. A few more kicks, and it was off its hinges. The ambulance jolted to a screeching stop. Both driver and passenger opened their doors and dived out of the ambulance, shouting and hollering. They slammed the doors shut. *Well, that's fucking rude.* Richard tried all the door handles, but he was locked in and on his own in the ambulance. Looking at the crumpled steel door of the cell he'd just broken out of, he eyed the tinted windows of the ambulance.

Annemarie followed the ambulance out of the hospital grounds. As they took the main road, the ambulance put on its blue siren and increased its speed drastically. Shaking her head and frowning at the necessity of this, she was soon left behind but kept calm. They were in the distance now, but she had her satnav and the address if she lost sight of them.

She was suddenly aware that the ambulance had its break lights on. The ambulance hit and mounted the traffic island in the middle of the road, tipping onto two wheels and then crashing down on four again. It came to a grinding stop, and bits of the bumper flew off. The front suspension and front wheel was all bent up, making the ambulance list to one side. Annemarie couldn't believe what she was seeing. *"Oh, my God! They can't even drive! Crashing like that with my son as a passenger! He could be hurt, being tossed around in that little cell.* As she got close, she saw the driver and front passenger exit the ambulance, running away from it. Both ran across the main road to get away from the ambulance. *What the fuck are they doing?* Pulling up alongside the ambulance, she got out and shouted to them, "What are you doing?"

"He's out, he's out!" they cried, clearly terrified and shaken.

She stomped round the ambulance to the side sliding

doors, anxious to see if Richard was OK. She tried the handle but it was locked, so she stood on tiptoes to peer into the ambulance's tinted window. She could see Richard holding what looked like a metal door over his head. He looked like he was going to use it to break the glass. She shouted his name.

When he saw her, he cried, "Mum!" He carefully lowered the crumpled metal door and then leaned it against the inside wall of the ambulance and came back to her. He sat on a seat.

"Are you OK?" she asked. "They've had an accident." Lowering her voice to convey her disgust, she added, "You'd think that they'd be better trained at driving fast. Are you sure you're OK, darling?"

Richard leaned close to the tinted glass. "I'm OK, Mum. I was worried that you couldn't keep up, coz you don't drive fast like that." Leaning over, he snagged a plastic bag from the front seat. Richard rooted in it and pulled out a packet of cheese and onion crisps with a triumphant "yay". He held them up for her to see. On the other side of the glass, she watched Richard munch his way through the crisps, demolish a chocolate bar, and then drain a carton of juice.

The police drove up, and after talking to the driver for a few minutes, a female officer cautiously joined Annemarie, who told the officer, "The ambulance had an accident while transporting my son to a hospital in Kent. The ambulance is locked."

The officer asked her if Richard was OK. After peering through the glass, Annemarie could see he was polishing off an apple and then putting all the food rubbish, including the apple core, back into the plastic bag, before dropping it back onto the front seat. He settled himself back on the seat near her, smiling at her through the window. It crossed her mind that he might have just eaten someone else's lunch, but she mentally shrugged and she told the officer, "Yes, he's fine."

Constable Dean was an experienced officer. After speaking to the private ambulance team, he joined his fellow officer at the side of the vehicle. He introduced himself and asked the patient's mother a few questions. Richard appeared to be calm, talking to the officers through the window. Dean asked him to stay seated while he got the ambulance door open. Richard's mum climbed into the van, going to her son and hugging him. They clearly had a good relationship. Constable Dean carried on, talking to the mother and son while they waited for a police van to transport Richard back to the hospital he had just left. After examining the empty cell, Constable Dean looked around and asked, "Where's the door gone?"

With a sheepish grin, Richard picked up the severely damaged door. Looking a little uncomfortable, he clarified the obvious. "I's a bit broke." He leaned it back against the inside of the ambulance. It wobbled a bit when Richard gave it a couple of sympathetic pats.

Constable Dean raised his eyebrows in surprise at the crumpled state of the steel door. While scratching his head, he wondered how on earth the boy had been able to completely kick it off its hinges. Admittedly, Richard looked strong, built like a rugby prop. But in all his years of policing, Dean had never seen anything like that.

The police van arrived, after watching mother and son hugging each other, Dean made the controversial decision to not use handcuffs on the patient. After some consideration, he asked the mother to lead her son into the police van cell, making sure to position the mum on the seat closest to the cell so that the patient could see his mother at all times. He escorted mother and son back to the hospital in the van while his colleague drove the mother's car. Thankfully all went smoothly, and Dean was able to hand the patient to the hospital staff without further incident.

It was still very early in the morning, and Annemarie had a sense of déjà vu as she waited outside the doors of the ward with Richard. The same sister unlocked the door. Annemarie was prepared for an argument, and she had no intention of leaving Richard with incompetent nursing staff. To her surprise and relief, the ward sister ushered them both into the ward. She led them to a sitting area which had tea and coffee, as well as a plastic-coated bench next to a small round coffee table. A different nurse gave Richard another couple of tablets with some water, and she carefully watched Richard as he swallowed them. Richard collapsed on the bench. He looked terrible: his T-shirt was sweat stained, his battered feet were filthy, and exhaustion had drained his face of all colour.

It must have been nearly 6 a.m., and some patients were getting themselves cups of tea. Annemarie was starting to feel in the way. She stopped a nurse and asked, "Where is Richard sleeping?"

The nurse pointed to the sticky bench on which Richard was unsuccessfully trying to fit his six foot sprawling frame. Annemarie pinned her with hard eyes, not even trying to hide her fury. She asked with a grim voice for a pillow and a blanket. When the duty staff nurse had told her there weren't any beds, she hadn't considered he meant there was literally nowhere to lie down. *What a total fuck-up.* The nurse came back with some bedding, and Annemarie took it from the nurse. She had been looking around and had spotted a day room that had leisure activities, but more important it two wide sofa benches. Pointing to the room, she said, "That room will be better. Richard is in the way of patients wanting to sit down and have their morning tea or coffee here." The nurse eyed Richard's frame taking up the whole area, with his dirty bare feet propped up on the coffee table, and reluctantly nodded. After unlocking the room, the nurse left her to her own devices. Annemarie took a few minutes to push the two large heavy sofas together, making a bed of sorts. Richard was already half asleep before his head touched the pillow, and she covered him up with the blanket. Annemarie squeezed next to him, lying on her side to watch over him. Her eyes became heavy, and sleep claimed her too.

She woke up with a start, her heart beating hard against her chest. She breathed out in relief when she saw her son sleeping peacefully next to her. She looked at the time on her phone: 8.20 a.m. Scribbling a note for when he woke up, she grabbed her things and quietly left the room.

Outside was a hive of activity. Patients, both men and women and from young adults to middle aged, were sitting in groups, drinking hot drinks, laughing, and joking. Some were pacing up and down the hallway in agitation. Others wanted to receive their medication and were lining up outside what looked like a stable door; the top half was open, and a nurse inside was giving each patient drugs in a tiny paper cup with some water. Some of the patients were sitting on random chairs, and they looked lost in their own thoughts, fragile and broken, with dark rings under their eyes. Others were impatient and fidgety, wanting to voice a complaint to anyone who was willing to listen.

Annemarie knocked on the nurse's office, and she could see through the soundproof glass that the staff were all new. *Day shift,* she thought. One of the nurses came to the door after first enquiring who she was from the ward sister. Annemarie was getting used to being looked at in that peculiar way, and it was a weird feeling, being evaluated by nurses who spent their working day assessing patients, weighing them up and trying to determine their frame of mind. She imagined it was a skill that became normal after a while working in this environment. However, to Annemarie it felt probing and alien. Speaking quickly, she gave them her mobile number and informed them she would be back at lunch visiting time, but they should call her if anything changed before then. The ward sister walked with her to unlock the double doors so she could leave. Bypassing the lifts, she ran down the stairs and through the main reception before stepping out into bright morning sunshine. She needed a shower and a strong coffee. Then she needed to pack a few basics for Richard and get herself ready to visit him at lunchtime.

Annemarie dressed in a yellow floral print skirt and a pretty capped sleeved white blouse. She wanted to look nice for her visit with Richard. After parking the car, she made her way to what was now becoming a familiar building. She signed in and then slapped a visitor sticker onto her blouse. She ran up the stairs, impatient to see her son. Richard was waiting for her by the double doors, and when he saw her through the strip of reinforced glass, he smiled and pressed his face to the glass, his nose squished flat. Annemarie was just as excited to see him. He looked fresh and clean, he his blue eyes were bright. He was wearing the cotton salmon pink pyjamas; she'd seen other patients wearing similar outfits that morning. Visiting time went quickly. She bought Richard clean T-shirts and shorts, some Converse shoes, his mobile, and a charger. Now they could talk whenever he wanted.

Annemarie was worried because the hospital still hadn't arranged a bed for him, but the staff reassured her that they would keep her informed of any developments. Richard was on strong antipsychotics and tranquilisers, and he really needed a room to rest to have his own space away from the other patients. The section 2 meant Richard would be detained for a minimum of twenty-eight days in hospital, and it was very unsettling to not know where or when he would be relocated. Mother and son hugged and kissed goodbye. Annemarie promised that she would visit him in the evening, and she reminded him that his sisters couldn't visit because the hospital had a "no one under eighteen" policy, but Richard's older brother, Andrew, said that he would come this evening as well. Going home without Richard was difficult and painful.

Annemarie got home, and she prepared pasta and green salad for the family to eat that evening, knowing that visiting time clashed with the usual time they ate. Annemarie spent another hour doing a bit of housework to keep busy before everyone else got home. She tearfully recounted all that had happened over the last twenty-four hours to the rest of her family. Andrew and the girls listened with mixed degrees of shock and dismay. Russell was appalled.

At 4.30 p.m., Annemarie gave the girls final instructions about dinner. Andrew was arranging to make his own way to the hospital at 7 p.m. She gave Russell a quick kiss goodbye and was at the front door when her mobile rang. It was Richard. *He probably wanted to make sure I'm on my way,* she thought.

"Hi, darling."

"Hi, Mum. Can you come and get me? I've left the hospital."

Annemarie's hand tightened on her phone, her stomach knotted with fear. She carefully asked, "Where are you?"

"I'm walking towards home," he said.

Annemarie stood as though petrified, her mouth open. A cold sweat of terror stood out on her brow. After giving Russell a panicked look, she said, "He's left the hospital!" She darted to her car, putting her phone on speaker so she could continue talking to Richard while driving. She was still eight minutes away when she heard the police sirens through Richard's phone.

Richard paced the corridor. The ward was quiet after visiting time, and patients wandered into their bedrooms. The nurses were writing up reports in the office. Richard continued to pace. He didn't have a bedroom to lie down in and listen to music, like he wanted. The chairs were uncomfortable, and the ward was hot and airless. He made a decision. He packed up his overnight bag, pocketed his phone, and marched to the fire exit. No one stopped him, and he used powerful kicks to force open the door. Sirens went off, alerting staff and security of his escape. After navigating down the external fire escape stairs, he ran around the outside of the hospital, scrambled over a wall, and landed near some wheelie bins. He ducked down behind them and then quickly changed from a black T-shirt to a grey one. Richard knew they had CCTV cameras posted around the hospital, and he hoped that changing his appearance would throw the police off his scent.

Walking sedately, he joined the throng of pedestrians on the wide footpath leading to the hospital's visitor car park, trying to appear nonchalant. He used his phone to call his mum and let her know he was making his way home. While striding down the main street, he continued to chat to his mother, reassuring her that everything would be OK. A police car drove past him on the opposite side of the road. He kept calm, his body language relaxed. Breathing deeply, he resisted the urge to run. Upon looking behind him discreetly, he saw the police car do a U-turn in the middle of the street, its blue lights flashing. Taking this as a sign that the chase was on, Richard broke into a run.

After turning onto a side road, he looked for a footpath or an alley that would leave the police vehicle unable to follow. The police sirens were blaring, and the vehicle was close on his heels. Then he saw what he was searching for. Richard dived down the alley, realizing he still had his phone by his ear, he quickly hung up on his mum's anxious voice. Legs pumping, he arrived at some garages at the back of a few houses. After pulling himself up onto a tall fence, he used it as a springboard to get onto the flat roof of the garages. Richard did a little strut across the roof and felt like the king of the world.

On foot now, the police had caught up to Richard and commanded him to come down. Richard lowered his overnight bag and his mobile to a female officer. She took it from him, trying to encourage Richard to come down. Instead, Richard moved back. He felt exhilarated, strong, and invincible. His body started to change on a cellular level, his breathing rate increased, and his muscles expanded and grew tense, ready for action. His pupils dilated as his body prepared itself to be more aware and observant of his surroundings. Mimicking a gorilla, he punched his chest. Richard jumped off the back of the garage, landing in a forward roll in someone's garden. After running through the garden, he vaulted over a gate separating the back garden from the front of the house. Jumping a low wall, he continued down the lane and past a village hall that led onto a recreational ground. Police sirens were loud behind him.

A police van screeched up by the village hall, and police officers jumped out, giving chase. Soon they joined by the other officers on foot. Richard sprinted over the grass field. Officers were flanking him on both sides. He remembered his rugby training and started ducking, weaving, sidestepping, and evading their grasping hands. Up ahead, he could see more police cars. Police officers were moving forward in a bid to intercept him.

Pulled up next to the police cars was his mum's little blue car, and she was next to it, waving frantically at him. She was like a ray of light to him. Changing direction, he barely avoided being caught, shrugging off the hands trying to bring him to ground. He ran towards his mum, his focus on her. He didn't see the officer who was using a police car as cover. That officer sprung out at the last minute with an extended baton, and he cracked it across Richard's shins, taking his legs out from under him. Richard tumbled to the ground, ending up face down in the grass, about ten metres away from his mum. Officers jumped onto his back and legs, shouting commands for him to put his hands behind his back.

Ignoring the shouts, Richard kept his arms tight, under his chest. He felt hands grasping his thick biceps, trying to force his arms out from under his chest. Richard squeezed tighter, shaking his head to the barrage of shouts and demands. When this was unsuccessful, the officers dug their knuckles into his side and into his backbone and neck. He could feel the pain just fine, and his shins were on fire, but it made him more determined. *That won't work, cunt. You've got to choke me out, motherfuckers.*

Through the shouts, he heard a soft voice calling his name, "Shush!" he thundered in the momentary silence. "Let me hear my mum!"

All eyes locked on Annemarie, and she swallowed audibly. In a low, soft voice, she said, "Can you put your hands behind your back, Richard? Please?"

"Yes, Mum." Richard pulled his arms out, and he was immediately handcuffed in a rough way. A few officers stood up. Now that Richard was restrained, they didn't need so many to hold him down, leaving four to sit and lay on Richard's lower back and legs. An officer strapped his ankles together to help keep him immobile.

One big, tall officer pointed a finger at Richard's prone figure and shouted at him. "You're lucky we didn't Taser you."

Annemarie was shocked that the officer should say something like this. She stomped up to him, looking a long way up to glare at him. "My son is not a criminal. How dare you suggest that you would Taser him!" Clearly showing her displeasure, she enquired, "Has he hurt anyone? Has he hurt any of you officers?"

"No, I haven't, Mum!" Richard piped up.

Crossing her arms over her chest, she raised an eyebrow at the flustered officer. The officer looked at his colleagues for back-up. That wasn't coming. Eventually he blustered, "He's given us all the run-around."

Annemarie could see all the police cars and the many officers that were needed to catch her son. With an earnest expression, she said regretfully, "I'm sorry about that, but it's important that you stay professional." She spoke quietly. "Richard has been given strong tranquilisers every four hours, by the hospital staff over the last two days. God knows how his body would react to being Tasered." Upset, Annemarie turned around, was finished with this conversation. She settled on the grass next to Richard's head, leaned over, and kissed his cheek. "Are you OK, baby?" While looking at Richard, who was face down on the hard ground, with police officers sitting and lying on top of him, she was suddenly very worried. "Can he breathe?" she cried. "People die while being restrained like this."

An officer sat next to her, showing her with his hands how the whole of Richard's back was free of pressure. The officers were sitting and lying on his hips and legs only. Nodding in understanding, she sat quietly next to her son.

They stayed like that, waiting for the hospital staff to decide what was going to happen to Richard. One of the officers, who was currently perched on Richard's butt, complained, "Look at my trousers." Tutting, he began brushing at the grass stains on his knees. While wiggling around to get a better view of the damage, he muttered, "These are my good pair."

Shock and emotional stress was taking its toll on Annemarie. She was incensed at the police officer's attitude while sitting on her son. His only concern was with his trousers! She was abrupt when she told the officer, "The police must be hard up for recruits, to employ such an ignoramus." Richard huffed out a laugh. Turning her attention to her son, she didn't see the officer be replaced by another. Later, she remembered seeing both officers—Taser and Grass Stain—talking to the senior officer. she never saw Grass Stain again, but Taser came back looking a bit sheepish and swapped with an officer who was putting pressure on Richard's legs. Maybe the only reason Taser was allowed to stay was because he was a big, tall, muscular officer and they needed him to help subdue Richard.

They waited like that for nearly an hour before hospital staff told the police to transfer Richard to a male intensive care psychiatric hospital (PICU) in Blackheath. The journey to Blackheath was horrendous. Police officers secured tight straps around Richard's knees and ankles. His hands were still handcuffed behind his back. Two officers helped Richard bunny hop to the waiting police van. Squatting low, Richard did a power jump to get into the back of the van. Once more he was put into a holding cell. One of the officers had parked Annemarie's car on a side road, and he told her it would be safe and wouldn't get a ticket for twelve hours. This meant she had plenty of time to arrange for it to be picked up by her husband and her oldest. Also, she could travel with Richard inside the van.

Annemarie sat on a seat close to the holding cell. Richard

could see his mum, but his thoughts became muddled. The vehicle drove fast through the traffic, the siren was loud and disorientating, and he could clearly see his mum's face white with worry. He stretched the bonds on his knees and ankles, and they started to become a little loose. His nose was dripping, and after wiping it on his sleeve, he was surprised that it was blood. He'd never had nosebleeds. It was so hot, and he was very thirsty and needed some water. Sweat ran down his neck, and trying to keep his balance was difficult. He couldn't hold on or brace himself to prevent himself from crashing around in the metal cell. They were taking him to prison, and the distress he felt sliced through him, like a serrated blade shredding his mind. He wouldn't be able to see his sisters. He would miss his Bruv. Tears stung the backs of his eyes. He couldn't remember what he had done, but it must have been serious. He looked sadly at his mum through the cage. Had he disappointed her?

Upon seeing his distress, she pressed her hand onto the reinforced thick plastic and metal cage. He pushed his forehead into cage where her palm rested. *This feels like torture,* Annemarie thought. Seeing her son losing his mind at the back of the police van, and not being able to help him, was brutal. She started thinking of other mothers who must have felt this kind of agony or worse—mothers who had lost their sons to drugs, alcohol, chronic illness, prison, accidental death, and murder. Young soldiers died in battle. Mary had seen her son crucified. Annemarie felt united to these unknown women and their suffering, and it gave her strength.

She turned to an officer who was silently watching their exchange. "How long before we get there?"

"Five minutes," he replied.

She knocked on the cage to get Richard's attention and told him, "Hold on," using a hand signal for five more minutes. She gave him a brave smile.

The police van pulled up outside the hospital. As soon as the side sliding door opened, Annemarie jumped out and ran to the back door, waiting impatiently while they unlocked and opened one side. Pushing the officer aside, she quickly clambered in and slid onto her knees in front of her bound son, hugging and kissing him. She was concerned about the bloody nose; it meant his blood pressure was too high. A water bottle was handed to her, and she unscrewed the bottle and held it to his mouth. He drank greedily, feeling instantly better now his mouth wasn't dry. The loud noise of the siren had stopped, and he could feel fresh air through the back door. His mum's arms hugged him close, and she said soothing words, reassuring him of her love. They had made it.

Two officers helped Richard jump to the entrance of the hospital. They got buzzed through the first doors and into a reception area. It was a brain-injury rehabilitation unit. Then a little way along the corridor, they got buzzed through the second set of doors, to a lift. There was only one floor up, and when the lift opened, this led to a foyer that had a tiny seating area with lockers. A tall, muscular man in his thirties named Stuart greeted them. The police officers helped Richard jump out of the lift, and Annemarie was told to put any personal belongings in the lockers. Stuart asked the police to remove the cuffs and release the limb restraints on Richard. One officer with a kindly gesture gave Annemarie Richard's overnight bag and mobile. She thanked him, but she was already preparing herself to enter the unknown world of an intensive care psychiatric ward.

Richard and Annemarie were buzzed through a third set of doors to an area that led to the fourth and final set of doors before entering into the intensive psychiatric unit (PICU). The open lobby entrance led to a long, wide traditional corridor, with patient rooms distributed along the corridor. Each room had a single bed and a wooden cupboard for clothes. Spaced along the corridor were shower facilities and toilets, which were kept locked until a patient needed to use them, and there was a large lounge area with comfortable seating and a huge wall-mounted TV. A dining area consisted of one long table with twenty high-backed chairs. There was a recreational area with a table tennis table, a treadmill, and a huge table to do arts and crafts. It also had the dual purpose of a staff meeting area. Richard and Annemarie were led away from the main part of the corridor and past a tiny reception that held a coffee table and two low, soft-cushioned chairs. They went into a large cold room which had bars at the windows. The hard, heavy furniture was nailed to the floor. It was an assessment suite, and high up in the corner of the ceiling, she noticed a vandal-proof, high-definition camera. Annemarie knew that this interview would be recorded. Stuart sat opposite mother and son, and an older female doctor joined him. They wanted to know as much history as possible. Richard's notes were being sent over; however, the doctor said she had what medication he was on. She was interested at how Richard had arrived at this point. Annemarie told her the whole sorry tale. The doctor looked tired, but she seemed kind and sympathetic. Richard was becoming increasingly more agitated, and he continuously watched the door, exiting to the corridor and only talking when questions were specifically directed to him.

Richard's bullshit radar switched on—a red alert light blinking like crazy. Were they playing some kind of game with him? The tall red-haired bloke was well muscled, and Richard sized him up at about ninety kilos; he didn't look like he lifted heavy weights, so Richard knew he was stronger.

The interview was nearly over. The doctor was getting up to leave, and Richard stood up and gripped his mum's hand tightly, pulling her slightly behind him as they followed Stuart down the corridor. Charlie Bronson was back. *You're playing with the big boys now, lad.* Down the corridor Richard walked, past many rooms. Most patients were standing or leaning in the doorways of their rooms, and they were interested in the new patient. They scrutinized him as he went past. Some patients smirked, and others left their rooms and followed the newbie and his mum down the long corridor.

Annemarie ran the gauntlet with her son, and it was the most intimidating experience of her life, walking past these young men. They didn't look like patients—they appeared to be bad boys—unpleasant young men who had experienced the harsh side of life. Annemarie tightened her hold on Richard's hand, looking down at her creased, grass-stained floral skirt and grubby blouse. She cringed at how she was so stupidly and inappropriately dressed. She stuck out like a sore thumb; a Sunday school teacher in a biker's bar couldn't have been more out of place.

They were shown into a room that contained a narrow

bed, one pillow, a thin blanket, no sheets, a plastic coated mattress, a broken wooden cupboard, and a small barred window that was nailed shut. Patients clustered together just outside the bedroom to gawp at the new boy. Annemarie's heart sank. This wasn't a hospital—this was a detention institution for the mentally and probably criminally insane. It reminded her of the film *Scum*. A couple of the patients were nudging each other and laughing. One in a hip-hop bandana murmured something about Richard's mum, and the one in the hoodie laughed, nodding.

Richard was watching, and he saw it and heard it. Then he went ballistic and savagely charged at the two men, getting aggressively into Bandana's face. He shouted, "That's my mum!" Richard's face was murderous as he roared, "Don't talk about her like that! Don't even fucking look at her, or I'll fucking have you!" He glared at the security staff, and his eyes watched every move Bandana and Hoodie made.

Stuart got between the patients, herding the two males away from Richard's room. Annemarie tried to calm her son down. His eyes were fierce, and his breathing was ragged. He wasn't listening, and he was pacing. She recognised the signs—his body seemed to grow, his brow lowered, and his fists clenching. After a minute, he seemed to become a little more controlled. Richard told his mum he was going to the toilet. He left his room, closed the door carefully after himself, and purposely shut his mum in the room. While stalking the male in the bandana, Richard's eyes were on his prey. He vaguely heard Stuart ask, "Are you doing this now?" He nodded, his lips pulled back to show teeth in a grim parody of a smile. His eyes were focused as he approached the male who had disrespected his mum.

Bandana didn't know what hit him. Richard moved quickly into Bandana's space, rage and aggression increasing his power and strength. He grabbed and lifted Bandana over his head violently slammed him onto the hard floor of the corridor. He leaned over the gasping male to get right into his face, his features tight with fury. With eyes like blue ice, he snarled, venom dripping from each word, "I'll fucking kill you."

The alarm was deafening. Shouts and cries were heard by the other patients and staff who'd witnessed Richard's attack on Bandana. Richard was dragged off Bandana and held down by six large security staff; two held his hands, bending them into a stressed position to keep him from moving.

The sudden sound of the alarm and the sound of Richard's loud roar gave Annemarie extra speed. She hurtled out of the room, skidding to a stop to see Richard face down again. Security and hospital staff held him still. Stuart lay flat on this stomach beside Richard, and he was holding one of his hands in a bent position and talking to him. Annemarie skirted round Bandana, who had landed on his back, the air driven from his lungs. She kneeled and leaned down so she could see Richard under the pile of bodies. She had no idea what was going to happen now.

She gave a little cry when she felt an arm as strong as a steel bar tighten round her waist and lift her up and away from Richard and the male staff. "Keep away. You could get hurt." She turned and met the concerned eyes of a young man who looked a lot like Bruce Lee: lean with whipcord strength. He had lifted her without any sign of strain.

They both froze when they heard the furious threat in

Richard's voice. "Get your fucking hands off her!" Danger poured off him, and icy rage made his blue eyes turn crystal. His narrowed stare gave a promised retribution.

"Uh-oh," Lee whispered softly under his breath. He passed her into Bandana's arms, whose eyes bugged in horror. Bandana quickly turned and passed her to Hoodie, as if she were a piece of hot coal. Hoodie gave her a dry smile and passed her onto the guy standing next to him.

She went down the line like that until she was thrust into the arms of a huge male nurse. She had to look a long way up to his large scarred face. He smiled calmly whilst leading her into a side room, gruffly saying, "Better stay here, miss, until we have things settled outside." After leaving her, he closed the door quietly behind him. Worry pressed heavily on her chest, tears pricked her eyes, and she paced, wringing her hands as the sense of a terrible weight of her loneliness crashed on her.

Thirty minutes later, Stuart came to escort Annemarie to Richard's room. Not unkindly, he suggested that she needed to go home. Richard was sitting on the bed, and he wanted his Mum to go home too. He quietly told her, "Mum, I can't do this with you here. I'm worried about you. Go home. I love you, but go home."

She swallowed her protests, held back tears, kissed him goodbye, and promised to visit him. She waved, giving him a brave smile as she left his room. Her expression immediately changed to become tightly drawn with worry and sadness. She was escorted by the big male nurse with the scars on his face, and they moved down the corridor and past the other patients. A thin, bony patient wearing tinted sunglasses hissed at her when she went past. "You've brought a devil in here. Your son is a devil."

Bandana punched him. "Shut it, C4. We've all been where he is." Annemarie stopped to apologise to Bandana, holding out her hand to shake his. Surprised by the gesture, Bandana's heart softened. "It's all right, ma'am. We all had a bad day when we first got here."

Annemarie's eyes flooded with tears at the boy's forgiveness. She felt humbled by it and thought to herself, *I'm not going to forget this. Thank you.*

"My name is Fritz," he said gently. "Try not to worry about him too much, ma'am. Things will get better."

She nodded and gave him a watery smile before she was ushered out of the two sets of double doors and left in the foyer by the lockers. After getting in the lift on her own, she made her way down, not stopping until she got outside, where she collapsed onto a bench and cried her eyes out.

Russell got a lift with his eldest son, Andrew, to pick up Annemarie's car. He tried to keep things going at home whilst Richard needed Annemarie, but honestly it was difficult. The last few days, he'd been going into work but had been functioning on autopilot. The girls were upset and confused and didn't want to go into school. It was as if a tsunami had hit his family. The mental health team, referred this period as "in crisis", and that was what it felt like.

Russell hadn't told Annemarie that while at work he'd had a phone call from Anthony Smith, a building contractor whom he had used in the past. Richard had worked as a labourer for the company for a time. Anthony quickly got to the point of the call. "I saw your nutcase son a few days ago." Russell grimaced, and his shoulders slumped. He ran his hand down his face, held the back of his neck, and sighed. "It's true, then. Annemarie told me that Richard said he saw you, but I was hoping it had been a figment of his imagination."

Anthony mockingly continued. "He was running around like a nutter, and he had an ironing board, stopping traffic and pretending to iron in the middle of the street."

Russell didn't appreciate Anthony's disparaging tone towards his son, and he tried to shrug away his irritation, replying in a stilted manner. "Well, you may be reassured that soon after you saw him, he got picked up by the police. They took him to a mental hospital. He has been sectioned and will remain in hospital for a while."

There was a stunned silence on the other end of the phone, Anthony's tone changed to shock and dismay. "God! I'm sorry, Russ."

Russell ended the conversation as quickly as possible. He felt gutted. He was trying to survive at work with a mortal injury, and he needed to go home.

Later that night, Russell felt Annemarie crawl into to bed. Her skin felt chilled to the touch, and he could smell her tears. He gathered her close and let her cry. Russell and Annemarie held each other all night. She whispered in the dark, telling him all about the police, the conditions in the PICU, and how Richard had attacked another patient. Russell shook his head in disbelief at the things he heard. Eventually, Annemarie fell into an exhausted, troubled sleep. He was worried about his wife; she seemed more fragile and was hurting a lot. He held her close to his heart. He knew she was a strong fighter, especially when her babies were threatened. This illness that Richard had was a huge threat, and Russell's concern for his boy ate at him all night.

Richard woke up to the unfamiliar sounds and smells of the PICU. He sat up, his eyes searching the gloomy, drab cell. His shoulders drooped in defeat. Dark thoughts crept into his mind like a black widow spider pretending to be his friend but instead entangling him in a web of lies and deceit. Uncertainty stretched before him like a gaping chasm. His heart pounded in his chest faster and faster. Adrenaline coursed through his veins. He'd never experienced this kind of fear—the knowledge that he was completely powerless, the realisation that his life was held by a single thread. Holding his head in despair, he hissed out a breath.

This ridiculous infatuation with Kim was childish, a teenager's dream. It embraced him in its arms while sucking the life out of him. Thoughts of her were never far from his mind. He felt stripped of all happiness, hope, and pride. He was like a knight in shining armour rushing to rescue the maiden in distress. Richard shook his head, trying to dislodge the grip of the spider's web wrapping around his mind. *She doesn't want you, Rich.* He felt poisoned by his love for her, sick to his soul. He was imprisoned by his deceptive thoughts, which took him down to the deepest dregs where he became only half a man. Distress rolled off him in waves. He looked out of the dirty little barred window wistfully. There was no hope in this black cave called despair. He needed to get out. A door encased in steel stood in front of him. He stared at it and didn't hear the murmurs around him—voices of staff and patients alike desperately trying to reduce his fright. He slammed into the door hard. The air burst out of his lungs as if he'd been punched in the gut by Mike Tyson, but he didn't care about that. His focus was on something greater than pain. This was an unstoppable force meeting an immovable object. Richard was the unstoppable force. No matter what happened, no matter the consequences, no matter if he died trying, he would continue slamming into the door over and over. He wasn't aware of his hands, his knuckles broken and the skin split wide, blood dripping from his clenched fists. With incredibly strong kicks, he attacked the wood framework the steel door was hinged on. Cracks appeared, and the sound of splintering wood encouraged Richard in his efforts. The heavy door was unhinged at the top and leaning to one side.

Hope blossomed in his chest—only to quickly wither and die as he felt strong hands grabbing his arms and legs, halting his movements. People gripped him hard around the waist. He frantically struggled, thrusting the hands away, but they were replaced by many more, determinedly forcing him onto the floor. Desperate, he cried out when they dragged him away from the door. His violent efforts to get free were to no avail. Slumped heavily in his captors' arms, Richard felt himself being thrown onto a hard mattress. Tablets were shoved into his mouth, and a cup of water was thrust into his hand. "Take the tablets, or we will give you an injection," a crisp, cold voice told him. After swallowing the tablets, Richard pushed his face into the pillow. He felt alone and terrible. An emptiness that couldn't be filled pushed him down, and tears gathered behind his eyes. Despair lashed him without mercy. His thoughts slipped away into a pool of darkness, and his eyes closed as oblivion took hold.

It was early. Annemarie stayed in bed while she listened to Russell get up and go downstairs. After pulling the covers over her head, she turned over onto her side and curled herself into a ball, bringing her knees to her chest. She rocked herself in agony too deep for words. Memories flooded her mind: Richard as a baby, his sweet smile and kind nature. Richard playing with his older brother, Andrew; the little boys had been so inseparable. Richard protecting his little sister Abigail from stinging nettles in the garden, or giggling uncontrollably at his sister's furious shouts while teasing her by stealing her doll. Six-year-old Richard propped up with cushions, feeding a bottle to his baby sister Emily while watching a show on TV. Richard playing the part of One-eyed Jack in the school production. Richard's first day at senior school; he looked so proud, walking with his older brother as both wore identical uniforms. Richard in his judogi, smiling. Richard running, swimming, laughing, and crying—a montage of memories that she kept in her heart. The grief she felt for her son was overwhelming.

She needed to get a grip on her emotions; hiding in bed and feeling sorry for herself wasn't helping. Plans needed to be made, and visiting time at the PICU started at 1 p.m. She intended to be at the hospital at 12.59. Her son was going to understand that he would never be alone and that his mother, father, brother, and sisters would always be there for him no matter how difficult things got. She set her jaw with determination, and her eyes were a steely blue. With a stiffened spine, she turned to her husband, accepting a cup of coffee he handed to her with a small smile of thanks. Fire burned and spat in her eyes as she caught his worried look.

Russell felt relief. He suppressed a grin and knew that look on her face; he had seen it many times. It usually meant someone was in trouble, and she was in battle mode.

Annemarie was it for him. He had fallen in love with her when he was sixteen, and his feelings had only grown over time. There was no one else he would rather have by his side. She was courageous, passionate, and funny, and he loved her with all his heart.

At 12.59 p.m., Annemarie patiently waited in the foyer. She had stashed her handbag in the locker provided. A large male nurse came out to meet her, and he was huge with massive shoulders, long muscular arms, and dark eyes set in a grim, hard face. He reached down to take the overnight bag she was holding. Without saying a word, he took out and inspected every item she had packed for Richard. Every piece of clothing was unfolded, pockets were pulled out, and the wash bag was emptied out onto the table. The snacks she had carefully packed were all pulled out and examined. The spray deodorant, a bottle of sports drink, and Richard's phone and charger were classified as contraband. After putting them in the locker with her handbag, she questioned the nurse about a mobile. He informed her that Richard would only be able to have a pay-as-you-go, call-only mobile—no photos, no Internet, no contract. They would keep the chargers in the office and charge any phone overnight for patients.

After the man gave her a quick scan to make sure she didn't have anything on her person, he led her through into the wide lobby. Striding towards Annemarie was a woman with a tense expression. Frowning at the nurse, she motioned her head towards the overnight bag Annemarie was holding. The male nurse gave a slight nod, and picking up on the nonverbal cues was easy. This woman was coldly assertive and dominant. Annemarie waited for the woman to introduce herself. She half smiled at the woman's calculating expression and stood perfectly still under her inspection, waiting to catch the woman's cool-as-ice look with one of her own. She sincerely hoped the "fuck you" was clear. It seemed to be a common trait in this type of environment to psychoanalyse anyone.

The woman pinned on a cold, formal smile, politely holding out her hand to shake. She introduced herself as the matron and informed Annemarie that Richard had tried to escape this morning. He had damaged a door in doing so and was now heavily sedated. She paused and then said in a cold, haughty voice, "You do realise that this is a psychiatric intensive care unit? Patients are very unwell here." She indicated the workman who was repairing a heavy, dented door.

Annemarie didn't understand or care what the matron was trying to say. She was sorry that Richard had caused damage again—but not that sorry. "Can I see my son, please?"

Irritated, the matron nodded her head, indicating that the nurse would show her the way. The matron paused once more to stress in a stony voice, "This is an intensive care unit, and visitors are not encouraged." Before Annemarie could reply, she dismissed her, turned sharply on her heels, stiffly marched into an office, and closed the door behind her.

Annemarie was led down the corridor. She was familiar with the layout now and knew where her son's room was located. Two members of staff were sitting outside his room, and the door was partially open. Annemarie pushed the door fully open and was shocked and dismayed to see Richard face down on the bare mattress. He was unmoving in a very heavy sleep. His hands were in a terrible state, swollen up. His stretched skin was black and blue, his knuckles were bleeding, and the skin had split on each knuckle.

Annemarie pushed the door, closing it a bit so it was only slightly open. She wanted some privacy with her son. After kicking off her shoes, she climbed onto the mattress beside Richard, sitting with her back against the wall. She touched his hair and face with soft fingertips, glad she was able to see him and be with him. The door opened wide, and she looked up from her son's face to see one of the staff indicating that the door needed to stay open so they could see into the room. Shrugging her shoulders, she let them get on with their job of staring at her while she sat with her son.

Richard woke up briefly and grumpily stared up into his mum's face. "You shouldn't be here," he mumbled before putting his head onto her lap, closing his eyes, and going back to sleep. They stayed like that for a long while.

She was aware of various people coming to peer at them through the open door, but she chose to ignore them. She did look up when she heard the matron's voice "Is she still here? She shouldn't be visiting him in his room." Her caustic tone was scathing in its criticism.

Annemarie could hear a deeper, quiet male voice answering reasonably. "Richard has had a strong sedative and is sleeping it off, so it is the only way she could see her son."

The matron's voice became stringent. "She cannot be in the patient's room, and that is final. Remove her. She can continue her visit in the assessment suite. If the patient isn't well enough for visitors, then she needs to go home and visit him another time."

Annemarie and Richard could hear the unnecessary fuss that was taking place just outside his door, and they shared a resigned look. With effort, Richard got off the bed, staggering around a bit until his legs got used to supporting his weight. He helped himself to one of the cartons of juice she had brought for him, made his way to the door, ignored the matron, and spoke with one of the staff assigned to monitor him throughout the day. "Where do you want us to go?" Annemarie walked next to Richard as he shuffled down the corridor. They were accompanied by the male nurse, who showed them where they could continue to spend time together.

Annemarie glared at the matron, and the mutual dislike was obvious when they locked eyes. Setting her teeth so she wouldn't shout at the stupid woman who'd derived much pleasure in being unaccommodating, Annemarie instead gave her a wide, fake smile and dismissed her as unimportant. The tiny room they were shown into was dismal, hot, and airless. There were no windows, and the walls were painted a horrible nicotine yellow. It had two low chairs and a small coffee table. No refreshments were available, and the room was extremely uncomfortable. It wasn't long before they were both perspiring from the heat. Annemarie spoke to one of the ever-present nursing staff and asked if there was another room where family members could visit patients. Annemarie was shocked to discover that visitors could only use the tiny room, or the assessment suite if it wasn't in use. Frowning, she wondered if they'd made it inhospitable on purpose to discourage visitors. Plus, it was obvious that only one patient and one visitor could fit in the room. When she got home, she was going to investigate the hospital. Cutting the visit short caused her pain, but the room was uncomfortable, and Richard was fading fast. Richard walked Annemarie to the lobby, waiting with her until a member of staff who was a keyholder came to let her out. After hugging him tightly goodbye, she left through the double doors.

On the wall was a board that had photographs of senior hospital staff, with their titles and names listed. Annemarie retrieved her mobile from the locker and took a photo of the board. Then she made her way out, deep in thought. She was not happy with the conditions of the PICU. She didn't expect it to be like a hotel, but she was unprepared with the lack of amenities and the hostile matron.

Richard saw his mum out. He watched her go through the double doors and disappear from his sight. His smile faded, and his expression turned solemn. His chest tightened, and he tried to control the fear he felt rising by breathing deeply. Two hospital staff followed him around to observe and monitor his behaviour; they were never far away but kept a discreet distance so he wouldn't feel crowded. He wondered if it was because he'd attacked Fritz or broken their stupid door. Or was this normal practice for new patients? He had watched TV programs and documentaries about what life was like inside prisons. This wasn't a prison, but the same rules applied—something about dominance, respect, strength, and becoming the top of the food chain. He kept himself alert, watching the other patients with suspicion. They kept a wide berth, not giving him any eye contact. They were obviously uneasy around him. Richard shrugged his shoulders. If they left him alone, that was fine by him. In his room, his mum had left him some supplies, snacks, and fresh clothes. Purposely ignoring the two shadows who sat outside his room, he pushed the bed to the far side of the room, giving himself some floor space to do push-ups. He could hear his two stalkers getting restless as they scribbled down stuff about him any time he moved. Maybe they were worried because he was rearranging the furniture. He flashed them a small smile, imagining what was on those clipboards *"At 4.05 p.m., he took a piss. At 4.20 p.m. he chewed some gum."* What a fucking boring job. Frowning, he looked around his room. He was going to miss lifting weights. There wasn't anything he could use as an alternative, nothing he could hang from to do pull-ups. *What would Charlie do?* Improvise by doing handstand press-ups. Richard's hands were swollen and damaged, so it was difficult to put his hands flat on the floor. His fingers were swollen and stiff. He couldn't bend them properly, but he managed to do thirty before his arms started to shake.

After jumping to his feet, he looked up to see Stuart leaning against his door frame, watching him with a sympathetic smile. Richard smiled back he hadn't seen Stuart since that first day. It was nice to see him, and he kind of liked the big lug.

"Missing the gym?" Stuart asked.

Richard nodded with a shrug. "I'm going to miss lifting."

Stuart straightened, shaking his head and giving him an apologetic look. "We have a treadmill, but no weights." Smiling, he patted Richard's shoulder in a companionable manner. "Come on. It's dinner time. I will show you where you can get something to eat."

Richard followed Stuart to the dining area. All the patients were queuing up and getting their plates filled with meat pie, vegetables, and mashed potato. It smelt good. Richard liked food, but not fancy stuff or anything with too much spice. He ignored the stares and the mutterings from the other patients; they didn't like him because he had attacked Fritz, who was a well-liked, leading member of the subculture within the hospital.

C4 continued to mutter and point at Richard; the man considered him to be the devil's spawn, sent to cause pain and destruction. Richard could hear him whisper chants and prayers against the evil stranger sent within their midst. C4 believed in demonic possession, and he kept his sunglasses on at all times to protect the windows of his soul. It was his duty to be a watchman, a prophet amongst God's people. Enemies could attack both spiritual and corporal, and therefore C4 needed to be guarded and ever watchful. This was why he was given the gift of insomnia. The doctors had prescribed many treatments to help him sleep, but they had all failed. He was resistant to sedatives and tranquillisers, and he believed that the unpleasant images he got were from God. He would quote scripture. Puffing up his chest, he bellowed, "In the last days, I will pour out my spirit on all flesh. Young men shall see visions." C4 preached that he was here for a purpose to eschew from sleep and to be ever watchful of evil.

Richard knew he wasn't evil, and it didn't matter how many times C4 said he was. He supposed C4 had a job to do, but he was looking in the wrong place, and if he carried on dancing around him and pointing his finger in his face, Richard would eventually would have to tell him C4 was batshit fucking crazy. *He's a different type of nuts to me,* he thought to himself.

Later that evening, before all the patients had their last meds, staff made a massive pile of toast with mugs of hot tea, which patients had while they watched a movie.

The next morning, a bloke introduced himself to Richard at breakfast. Steve was an ex-soldier in his early thirties, and he spoke nice and calm. He was being friendly because he knew Richard was being shunned by the others, and Steve wasn't having any of that. Rich was just a kid, built like a brick house, but he was still a kid. Steve had heard all the talk about how Richard had thrown Fritz down like he was nothing.

When Steve asked Richard about it, the kid got riled up quick, saying, "He should never have said that about my mum, then, should he? No one talks about her like that."

This boy sure loved his mum. It made Steve realise it'd been a while since he'd called his own mum. As he got up to leave, he shook Richard's hand. With a friendly smile, he advised him, "Keep it cool and calm, listen to your mum, and do what she says. Then everything will be good like tomatoes, yeah?"

Richard nodded wisely. "Yeah." Richard's hands were very sore and were still swollen and busted up. He flexed them open and closed, trying to ease the stiffness of his fingers as he walked down the corridor to his room.

The little guy who looked and moved like Bruce Lee stopped to talk to him, Richard had seen him last night deliver a flying kick to the head of a patient. The guy wasn't doing anything—he was just sitting there, watching the movie. Lee took him out and then almost busted a gut laughing so much. He found it hilarious, but his laughter died a quick death when the patient got up off the floor, rubbed the back of his head, glared at Lee with a death stare, and started to lumber like a giant bear towards him.

Richard inadvertently got in his way. Without any sign of effort, the guy lifted and moved Rich aside easily as if he was a child, muttering a low "'Scuse me." He pointed at Lee and growled a threat. Lee screeched a high-pitched, girly sound and then ran out of the room. Richard shook his head. These people were insane.

Studying Lee now, Richard could see no evidence of injury. He must have escaped. If that guy had gotten hold of him, he could have snapped Lee like a twig, Lee indicated Richard's hands and advised, "Keep hands flat—don't make fists. Heal better that way."

Richard muttered a gruff thanks and watched Lee as he sauntered down the corridor the opposite way. In his room, he started to do push-ups, sets of one hundred, until he felt tired. Mum said she'd be visiting today. All of a sudden he felt sad. Grimacing, he made himself do more push-ups and then flung himself onto the bed, looking up at the cracked ceiling. His eyes grew heavy, and thankfully he let himself slip back into sleep for a while.

It was 1 p.m., and Annemarie was in the foyer. A member of staff unhurriedly looked through the items she had brought with her. She'd noticed how thirsty Richard had been yesterday, and it made sense to her. She noticed a patient asking for some water; he was talking to a nurse through a hatch built into the wall of the staff office. It had a sliding glass panel, and this was where the patients also requested their mobile phones after they'd been charged. Sighing with a resigned expression on his face, the patient leaned against the wall, having no other choice. He was willing to wait for a drink of water. Annemarie gave the patient a sympathetic smile as she went past.

Today, Annemarie had bought with her litres of bottled water and juice. She wanted to make sure that her son wouldn't have to beg the matron for breadcrumbs. Really, she mused, the ward should have some sort of water-filtered fountain so that patients could help themselves to water when they wanted; especially because they were all on strong medication, it was even more important to stay hydrated. The system at the moment was inconvenient. The patients had to ask for water, and the staff members would have to stop what they were doing, unlock the kitchen, fetch the patient a plastic cup of water, and then lock the kitchen back up. Or the patient would simply have to wait to have his thirst relieved until the staff had the time to do it.

She had also brought as a change of clothes, more snacks, fresh fruit, and a pay-as-you-go mobile. Annemarie had bought with her some of Richard's bedding. Yesterday, she'd discovered that he was still sleeping on a bare mattress, and his comfort was important to her. The staff member queried Annemarie about the bedding, and she told him that her son was sleeping on a bare, sticky plastic mattress and a flattened, coverless foam pillow, so she had brought some bedding from home. She gave him a sweet smile and fluttered her eyelashes at him innocently. He was frowning, but she saw his lips twitch as if he was hiding a smile. Sighing, he shook his head at her. "I will have to ask the matron if he is allowed the bedding."

Nodding, Annemarie flatly replied, "Yes, you do that."

Richard slowly came down the corridor, Annemarie was shocked at his appearance. His frame was slumped, his shoulders drooped, and his head seemed too heavy to be supported by his neck because his chin rested on his chest. Instead of walking one step in front of the other, he dragged his feet as if had concrete blocks attached to them. Brushing off the nurse's restraining hand, she ran down the corridor to meet him halfway. Linking her arm through his, she smiled and greeted him warmly as if everything was OK. They shuffled like this together as they followed the nurse into the assessment suite. Visiting times were long, and she was prepared for an uncomfortable four hours. The chairs were hard and weighted in such a way that they were difficult to push close together, Annemarie pushed one chair close to the long bench that was fixed to the wall. She got Richard to lie down on the bench while she sat close, holding his hand. After kicking off her tennis shoes, she propped her feet up on the bench, getting as comfortable as possible while she waited for Richard to recover from the strong medication they must have just given him. At least she was prepared. She had a thermos cup of coffee and had made some lunch to eat, with extras for Rich if he wanted some. It looked like he needed to sleep more than anything. There was no doubt in her mind that this was caused by some very powerful tranquilisers.

It didn't surprise Annemarie that within ten minutes, the matron made an appearance. Keeping her body relaxed and her expression neutral, the matron gave her a bored look when she explained with an anal tone how Richard could not have the bedding from home. They use special, fire-resistant bedding.

Interrupting her little spiel, Annemarie enquired, "Do you intend to provide him with some, then?"

Annemarie knew about the camera, and she saw the matron tilt her head towards the camera high in the corner of the ceiling. She gave it a quick glance. Huffing as if Annemarie was being completely unreasonable, the matron explained that all rooms were cleaned and bedding changed daily. The reason she had seen his bed without bedding on was because her visit to see Richard had interrupted that process.

Annemarie held her breath, she was watching this woman carefully. If indeed lightning did strike liars, the matron would be a smoking husk right now. She gave the matron a small, cynical smile, her eyes bright with scepticism. She decided not to answer and could only hope that now the subject had been brought up and caught on CCTV, Richard would get some bedding. Either way, she had done the best regarding that matter. She looked down at her son, running her hands softly through his hair while he slept. On purpose, she turned her back on the matron to dismiss her. The matron cleared her throat. Then with a persuasive note in her voice, she said that Richard would be more comfortable sleeping in a bed, so maybe she should visit some other time.

Annemarie frowned up at the matron and spoke sharply. "Has something happened this morning with Richard?"

The matron shook her head, a bit surprised by her question. "No," she replied with a confused expression.

Annemarie looked straight at the camera and paused, clearly showing the matron that she'd known all along that the CCTV camera was monitoring the conversation. She explained innocently, "Richard is very sedated, and I'm questioning the necessity of this, especially if there hasn't been an event that warrants him being on such strong tranquilisers."

The matron stiffened, stiltedly replied that she would let the doctors know about her concerns, and left the room without further comment. Annemarie sat back in the chair and made herself relax her shoulders. While sipping her coffee, she narrowed her eyes over the rim and smiled grimly.

Richard was able to receive calls from other members of the family. Annemarie had left him a mobile with twenty pounds' worth of texts and calls on it. He wondered why he needed a burner phone. Maybe she knew they were monitoring his phone calls again. She had also stocked him up with a huge supply of bottled water and snacks. It crossed his mind that he should listen to the news. Perhaps she was expecting a nuclear attack from the Russians. He sighed and thought about Putin and a possible World War III. It was great hearing his younger sisters' voices; they couldn't come and see him because they were both under eighteen. Andrew, his older brother, was visiting him at 7 p.m., and his mum had visited this afternoon. His memory of it was vague and hazy. His dad had promised to call him before bed tonight, and Layla, his cousin who lived in Isle of Wight, was going to call him every day too.

The next day, Annemarie was in the foyer, waiting to be let in. Through the square panel of reinforced glass, she could see Richard waiting for her. He'd given her a call when she was parking the car, so he knew she was on her way up to see him. As she came through the double doors, he greeted her with a big hug, sweeping her off her feet. He boomed, "Hi, Mum!" He looked so much better today; his eyes were still a little dull, but the heaviness of sedation wasn't present. When they were let into the assessment suite, he told her that he had spoken with Dad and Layla, and he'd loved seeing Andrew. He told her that he wanted to go home with Andrew. When they'd said goodbye last night, he had felt sad at seeing him leave. Then Sonny cheered him up. It was pizza night, and another movie played. Sonny sat with Rich, whereas most of the other patients were still cautious of him because of what had happened with Fritz. Sonny took time to befriend Richard, and his natural, positive personality gently guided Richard in adjusting to his surroundings. Later, he had confessed to Rich that at first he had felt frightened about approaching him. Richard didn't understand because he would never hurt anyone. Richard lifted his chin up, puffed out his chest, and said he was a gentleman.

Richard introduced Sonny to his mum, and Sonny asked permission to call her Mum too. Sonny was lovely, kind, and sensitive. He was nearly at the end of his treatment, and he'd be going home to his family in a week or two. Richard told his mum that he was missing lifting weights. He said, "I miss it so much, Mum. Can't you bring in some dumb-bells for me? I could do some curls, shoulder presses, and exercises. It would make me feel good. Can't you ask them if you can?"

Annemarie knew they wouldn't let him have anything like heavy metal weights in a psychiatric hospital. Instead, she said she hoped he wouldn't be here long, and when he came home, he could use his home gym whenever he wanted. Richard was clearly disappointed and getting a bit stressed that he couldn't do his normal fitness routine.

Annemarie worked at getting him out of hospital. She'd

gotten some advice from a solicitor, and she was going to use her parental powers as Richard's nearest relative to challenge the section 2. At home, she was composing a letter to write to the team of doctors at the PICU. She had already informed her work of the situation, and for the moment she had been signed off from work. In her heart, she knew this was a life-changing condition for Richard which would greatly impact the family.

Richard was doing handstand press-ups and now wanted to do some squats. He said, "Mum, climb on my back. I want to do some squats." She stood on the bench so she could easily climb onto his back, hanging on like a monkey while Richard squatted using her weight as resistance.

He had completed about twenty squats when the door was thrust open, and in marched a very indignant matron. "Stop! Get off him!" she commanded.

Annemarie slipped down onto the floor and stared at the matron. Richard looked down and blushed as if he was guilty and been caught doing something terrible; all of a sudden, he found the floor very interesting. Looking at Richard's naughty-boy expression made Annemarie get the giggles. She felt a bit embarrassed and tried to hide her amusement behind a hand. The matron glared at Annemarie, furious. "This is a psychiatric intensive care unit. You should not be stimulating my patient like this!" She pointed an angry finger at the camera. "Your behaviour is being monitored and is unacceptable. This is why we don't encourage visitors at the hospital."

Annemarie felt herself bristle. She stepped towards the matron, crossed her arms over her chest, and gave her the death stare. Richard ducked behind his mum, keeping low and trying to make his hulking frame disappear. The atmosphere and mood in the room had changed swiftly. With a loud, cold bite to her tone, Annemarie addressed the matron. "That's not what your website says." In a mocking voice, she used air quotes. "'We recognise the vital role family and friends have in supporting patients in their recovery, and we actively encourage visitation from anyone who would like to visit.'" Her eyes shot fiery darts at the stunned matron. "However, I think you're right," she said sarcastically. "The website says is a pack of lies, because you have actively discouraged me from visiting my son every day." She was raging. "The facilities you have for visiting are extremely poor. You give us a choice of a stone-cold assessment suite which monitors our time with our loved ones with a CCTV camera, or if that's already in use, a poky, airless, cramped room little bigger than a utility cupboard in which only two people can fit." While ticking off on her fingers, she seethed. "There's nowhere we can get refreshments. You don't have a vending machine, a water fountain, nothing! And regarding the piggyback squats he was doing, that's me trying to help my son stop stressing, because he misses exercising, especially weight lifting. It's not to stimulate him, but to give him some normalcy."

By now the matron had paled and looked sick. She was opening and closing her mouth like a fish. Richard sidestepped cautiously towards the door. Annemarie felt hostile and full of anger. She couldn't remember disliking anyone as intensely. After taking a deep breath in, she blew out slowly. This wasn't good for Richard. She needed to get a grip on her emotions. The matron left muttering something about how she would pass on her comments, and then she made a hasty getaway.

Richard peeped at Annemarie to see if it was all over. Releasing a breath, Annemarie realised the afternoon had been a disaster. Some of the patients had heard her shouting at the matron and had congregated outside the door to listen. When the matron had left the room, storming down the corridor, they'd crept forward looking into the room to see if the coast was clear.

Sonny broke the tension by saying, "Wow, Mum. You sure told her!"

Richard grinned and mock punched Sonny in the arm. There was laughter from a few staff and patients, and just like that, the storm was over.

Over the next few days, Annemarie continued to visit Richard in the afternoons and filled the evening visitations with friends and family. She spoke to her vicar, and he agreed to visit Richard as well. He spoke to Annemarie afterwards. Apparently he was just leaving after praying with Richard when a member of staff pointed out a line of patients who wanted prayer as well. The vicar was so moved when praying for the young men in the hospital that he started visiting the hospital every evening, not leaving until all who wanted prayer received it. It didn't take long for Annemarie to realise she was the only parent visiting her son in the afternoons, so she got in the habit of bringing in little treats for all the boys as well as her son: sweets, multiple bags of crisps, trays of doughnuts, ice popsicles, and slices of watermelon (C4's favourite). The visits from the vicar convinced him that indeed Richard was not evil after all.

It wasn't long before all the young men were calling her

Mum, waiting for her to arrive at 1 p.m. with treats and a warm smile. The patients accepted Richard and no longer avoided him. Sonny and Richard became inseparable. Annemarie was very aware that Sonny's discharge date was looming, and she wanted Richard to be put into her care as soon as possible, especially because she knew that not having Sonny with him would make life in the PICU intolerable.

Things continued like this for the next week. The matron kept a low profile, and she never spoke to Annemarie again, preferring to use her staff to give her any information regarding Richard.

Then one afternoon as Annemarie was leaving the hospital, a member of staff gave her a letter. With trembling hands, she opened it. The doctors and hospital management had agreed to meet with her to discuss her petition to accept responsibility for Richard's care. It was for the following Thursday. It was good timing because Friday was Sonny's leaving party, and on Saturday morning he would be discharged. Annemarie hoped the meeting would go well and Richard could be discharged early; he was about halfway through his section 2.

Thursday, the day of the meeting, Annemarie waited in the small visiting room with Richard. A few other patients had important meetings with the PICU management as well. A male nurse came into the room, smiling reassuringly, and in a chipper voice said, "Here's your medication, Richard." Richard took the pills with a wordless nod.

Annemarie frowned. It was unusual for Richard to have medication at this time. It was 1.45 p.m., normal afternoon visiting time, and he'd never been given medication at this time before. It didn't take long for Annemarie to realise that the medicine was patient preparation for the coming meeting. Richard had started to melt, and his body went completely lax. His expression was open and childlike.

One of the nurses on the team came into the room, and mother and son stood up together, expectant. With an apologetic smile, the nurse said, "We want to talk with Richard first, if that's OK. Then I'll come to get you to join us very soon."

Annemarie frowned as Richard gave his mum a beaming smile. "It's going to be fine, Mum. Don't worry." He gave her a quick kiss on the cheek and bounded after the nurse. Annemarie was left alone.

The door to the room was ajar, so she overheard voices talking just outside the room. It was Fritz talking to a member of staff, and he sounded very upset. He'd just come out of his meeting, and things hadn't gone well. "They're keeping me in. Man, I done my time, but they say they're extending me on a section 3. Why? That's three to six months! Why have they done that? I've already done three months. I haven't seen my daughter for ages—she's a baby. Fuck, man. Why did they do that? It's not fair." Fritz sounded hopeless and broken. Annemarie's eyes flooded with tears at the pain and suffering in the young man's voice. Her chest got tight with emotion and fear that the same might happen to her son.

The nurse came for Annemarie forty minutes later. She entered the conference room. Eight people sat round a table. Annemarie's confused eyes met her son's guileless face. She could sense laughter and light-heartedness in the air, as well as amusement coming from the strangers. It was unexpected. Annemarie knew her son was wonderful. *The medication must have helped reveal it for all to see,* she thought. Richard greeted his mum with his usual enthusiasm. He made sure she sat down safely, and then he loudly scooted his chair as close as possible to hers, holding her hand. He proudly introduced her to the smiling team.

The questions directed to Annemarie were abrupt. She did her best to alleviate their concerns by informing them she intended to give up work and become his full-time carer. When Annemarie felt defensive about the more intrusive questions, Richard was quick to reassure his mum in a wise, old-man tone. "It's all right, Mum. They just need to ask these questions coz they don't know us." He patted her hand and smiled, his eyes twinkling merrily. She turned her confused gaze to the team and saw them hide smiles and soft chuckles.

The most senior doctor cleared his throat to get everyone's attention. "I think we need to come to a decision about whether we agree to release Richard into his mother's care. Can I have a show of hands, please?" Just like that, it was over. Richard was coming home. To give them time to arrange support for Richard in the community, his discharge day was set for the following Monday.

Richard and Sonny spent a lot of time together. They exchanged phone numbers, and the last few days went slowly for both of them. Fritz was understandably disgruntled that Richard was going home after only two weeks. Richard overheard him complaining to a member of staff, "How come he gets to go home? He slammed me to the floor! I have to stay, but he gets to go? It's got something to do with his mama causing trouble and getting that preacher in to pray and stuff, doesn't it?"

Richard shrugged his shoulders indifferently as he

walked away. He knew he had a good mum, and she was getting him out on Monday.

The hospital had arranged for a taxi to collect them. Russell dropped her off at the hospital because she wasn't allowed to drive Richard home herself; however, she could accompany him in a taxi. *Some sort of hospital policy.* Richard opened the taxi window, closing his eyes to feel the warm wind brush his face. The sunlight gleamed through the trees as they sped past. He was going home! Tears slipped down his cheeks as he felt overwhelmed with gratitude.

Annemarie watched her son with tears in her own eyes. She was bringing her son home, and that was all that mattered. As for the rest, they would take it a day at a time.